HARLEY-DAVIDSON

HARLEY-DAVIDSON

MALCOLM BIRKITT

First published in 1992 by
Osprey Publishing Limited,
59 Grosvenor Street, London W1X 9DA

© Malcolm Birkitt 1992

Cataloguing in Publication Data for
this title is available from the British Library

ISBN 1 85532 204 8

Editor Shaun Barrington
Page design Angela Posen
Printed in Hong Kong

Front cover
*Classic view of a classic bike – the
Harley-Davidson Electra Glide
Classic, in fact. Enough power and
comfort to carry a rider and
passenger, plus all their luggage,
anywhere they wish. Makes you want
to head for the hills. The electric-
starting FL – called the Electra Glide –
first appeared in the early
1960s.(David Goldman)*

Half-title page
*A clear road, inviting bends, tree-clad
vistas and sunshine, this must be Hog
Heaven. Actually it's near Aspen,
Colorado. (Mac McDiarmid)*

Title page
*Catching some rays and watching the
parade at Daytona.*

For a catalogue of all books published by Osprey Automotive
please write to:

**The Marketing Department, Octopus Illustrated Books,
1st Floor, Michelin House, 81 Fulham Road, London SW3 6RB**

Contents

Japanese custom and retro-bikes come and go, but in the style-conscious 1990s, only Harley-Davidson would dare produce a motorcycle like this

Introduction

Alongside the word 'Mom', what American brand-name do grown men tattoo on their chests and biceps? Which American company has one of the world's longest surviving marques? There's only one answer to both questions – Harley-Davidson. Founded back in 1903, and having survived rocky times recently, the USA's only remaining volume producer of bikes is now basking in cult-like status. Its machines are right up there with apple pie and the Statue of Liberty in American mythology.

Each and every machine adorned with the revered H-D badge is almost a piece of metal sculpture. With a big, booming V-twin engine for propulsion, these bikes give riders a unique feeling of pride, power and individual freedom – the latter in some ways a particularly significant concept for the American people. So well defined is this image that the major Japanese manufacturers have been falling over themselves for years attempting to imitate the Harley 'look', or to achieve a fraction of its marque devotion. In both objectives they've met with strictly limited success.

In North America, motorcyclists often seek to make a statement about style and individuality, or show that the latest Oriental solution to two-wheel problems isn't necessarily the best one. Invariably they choose a home-produced bike designed and crafted by human creators with an eye for tradition – not one of the sleek but largely anonymous imported machines created by a phalanx of computers and mass produced by armies of robots.

The bikes which currently roll off Harley's assembly lines are, compared to the sophistication and complexity of large-capacity Japanese machinery, technically outmoded and way behind in terms of performance and efficiency. However they are ideally suited to American riding conditions. Though the Milwaukee-based irons are no slouches, few buy a Harley for its maximum speed – they actually work better the slower you go! In addition, twisty bits of tarmac soon reveal relatively modest scratching ability, and stopping power in standard trim isn't recommended for those of a nervous disposition. Despite these fundamental deficiencies, Harley Davidsons are accorded almost divine status by hordes of American and Canadian bikers seeking a certain style of two-wheel transport.

Patriotism only partially explains Harley's popularity. Despite an often poorer climate for motorcycling, the H-D cult has survived the ocean crossing to Europe intact, bringing a new dimension to the traditional 'big-bore twin' scene previously dominated by machinery from BMW, Ducati & Moto Guzzi. As in the USA, cruising around on a Harley-Davidson is now very much the thing to do, and be seen doing.

Whichever side of the Atlantic you care to examine, the Harley -Davidson phenomenon is as much about the characters who ride the machines as the actual bikes themselves. The archetypal dude with a full beard sat astride his customised hog may well be a modern day rebel, but it's just as likely he's a computer programmer, lawyer or business executive these days. Appearances can be mighty deceptive because, just below the fierce exterior many Harley riders adopt, are some of the nicest people you could ever meet. This book is a tribute to their comradeship, vitality, and love of motorcycling aboard the all-American legend.

Equally, words of appreciation are due to many individuals whose co-operation and assistance in this project have been invaluable. I'd like to pick out Nicole and Tom Barnes of Houston, Texas, ace snappers Mac McDiarmid and David Goldman, both from London, and Roger Winterburn of H-D dealers Windy Corner, Barwell near Leicester, for special thanks.

Below
The archetypal Hog rider in the flesh –
Dangerous Don patrols the coastline
on his elderly FLH

Cruisin 'n' posin – all part of the
Harley-Davidson experience

Recurring custom themes interwoven with the Harley name are also symbols of American patriotism – the Stars and Stripes, and more eagles than you'll ever see in the wild

*Small gas tank, big V-twin, springer
front forks, masses of chrome – it
could only be a Harley-Davidson*

Two big, old-fashioned Harley steeds,
designed to fit the grand scale of the
American landscape, line up in Old
Dodge City. (Mac McDiarmid)

How about this for a personal plate!
Roy brought his bike all the way from
cold California to sunny old
Cheltenham, England

The American flag forms a fitting backdrop to Harley's latest reincarnation – the Sturgis. Named after an annual motorcycle rally in the Black Hills of South Dakota, the bike shows how this unique motorcycle maker moves forward yet keeps an eye on its past. The low-slung lines of the Dyna Glide chassis echo compact proportions of older rigid-mount machines. (Mac McDiarmid)

Wherever you look – even in your mirrors – there's no forgetting which bike you're riding

Origins

When three men named Davidson and Mr Harley produced their first motorcycle back in 1903, little did they know that a future American institution had just been created. Certainly they could not have foretold the fluctuating fortunes of the company, nor the precipitous events eighty years after the company's formation: when in 1985 Harley-Davidson, plagued by financial difficulties, almost became a historical footnote, and the USA came within a whisker of losing not just its entire domestic motorcycle industry, but also a cherished national symbol.

The Indian marque – now resurrected and back in low volume production – had departed the scene as a major manufacturer by the mid-1950s. Three decades later the Milwaukee-based concern, formed shortly after the turn of the twentieth century, was literally hours from the threat of bankruptcy when its rescue deal was hammered out.

As bike sales boomed in the early 1970s, AMF – Harley's parent company – ordered such an increase in production that standards slipped badly. By the end of that decade, the motorcycle division was suffering from poor quality control, troublesome mechanicals, increasingly stiff competition from the East and a general malaise in the bike industry. Harley-Davidson sales had slumped by the early 1980s to an alarming low point, and its reputation had plummeted.

Diminishing numbers of people, it seemed, were suffering the irritation of kerbside repair, or having to push or transport their bikes home after yet another breakdown. For those with Harleys that kept running, the sight of engine oil dripping all over their driveways was of little consolation. Dealers with H-D franchises were continually besieged by warranty work.

What a contrast to the current situation! Not only are the machines oil-tight, but the reliability problems have been eliminated. A new engine, still in the time-honoured V-twin configuration of course, has breathed fresh life into the company, and component and assembly quality has been radically improved. Yet none of the

An immaculate Shovelhead, cleaner than the day it left the factory twenty years ago, carries rider and passenger out for an evening blast

Above
This well-preserved Shovelhead FLH looks like it might chug on for ever. The rack cum passenger perch looks like it gives you a hard time, though

Right
The age of a Harley is almost immaterial, because the 'look' remains more or less the same. Though the rider of this sidevalve 45 – once made in plentiful numbers but now a collector's piece – does sport a fetching pudding basin helmet. (David Goldman)

essential character or traditional flavour of the bikes has been lost. On top of all this, financial stability has returned as the company first wrestled clear of AMF control, then went public on the stock market. Despite the economic downturn, Harley's profit graph – once diving towards the floor – has quickly recovered. Despite a recession in the UK, British sales have shot through the roof.

Though only accounting for 15% or thereabouts of the lucrative American market – the Japanese big four dominate it – the bikes built by Harley-Davidson have created a niche all of their own, and one that looks impregnable. Many motorcyclists are reacting against a period of overly complex oriental machinery, and joining those who already appreciate the elemental nature of a Harley, value its sense of tradition, or just love the image it confers on a rider. Though they arrive at the same conclusion from different starting points, each group of bikers acknowledges there is simply no alternative to the American legend.

It's no surprise, given this context, to learn that for the last 35 years the type of machines made by Harley-Davidson has hardly altered, though a series of technical enhancements have been introduced when necessary. The range still comprises entry-level Sportsters with a smaller-capacity V-twin, plus the bigger-engined custom and cruising models, and finally the heavyweight tourers. In American minds, weight still suggests quality, and the Harley has plenty of each.

While the Japanese continue to explore the outer limits of performance, and juggle with countless permutations of design, Harley-Davidson stick to what they know best. With bags of chrome, a shapely petrol tank and the classic, air-cooled V-twin engine supported by a tubular steel frame, Harleys have always looked and sounded like real motorcycles. No doubt the company management will keep them that way, if they have any sense.

Many regard Willie G Davidson, grandson of one of the founders and currently Head of Styling, as the real caretaker of the Harley heritage. Though an executive in his late '50s, his full beard, longish hair and casual clothes perfectly fit the typical Harley rider stereotype. Ever willing to mingle with and talk to ordinary bikers across America, his public pronouncements reassure us that, while progress is being pursued, the bikes will continue to embody Harley-Davidson's 'special essence'.

The AMF corporation's control of Harley-Davidson, which ended in 1981, was an unhappy chapter in the marque's history. Attempts to boost production, to keep up with the market boom of the '70s, meant the bikes were plagued by poor quality control and chronic mechanical problems

Above

Resplendent in its dazzling white and grey paint scheme, this Shovelhead-engined Electra Glide has been tastefully customised and given the benefit of some decent carburation

Right

Between the Sportsters and the FLs, Harley makes a host of stylish and factory-custom models, typified by this Heritage Softail Classic. Middle of the range, not the middle of the road

The motorcycle you see here was ridden by the hero of "Bebop Bamboozled" the halftime show of Super Bowl XXIII between the Cincinnati Bengals and the San Francisco 49'ers. Harley-Davidson built 107 motorcycles featuring the Super Bowl XXIII graphics of 1989.

As much a part of American culture as the Empire State Building – that's Harley-Davidson's Heritage Softail. This version, a limited edition 1989 model residing in the Harley museum alongside its York, Pa factory, made a celebrity appearance at the 23rd Superbowl. (Mac McDiarmid)

Harley's King of the Highway – that's the Electra Glide Classic. Generous footboards are fitted front and rear to all the big FL tourers

V For Victory

Harley-Davidson and the V-twin engine – the terms are now virtually synonymous. So it may come as a surprise to learn that the first ever motorcycle produced by this marque back in 1903 employed just a single cylinder motor. But the V-twin layout, adopted six years later, has been a Harley hallmark ever since. How come? Simply because this engine configuration is light, compact, efficient and ideal for the proportions of two-wheelers. It has served the Milwaukee outfit well for over eighty years, and happily its future looks assured for many years to come.

While the Japanese big four rapidly perfected the multi-cylinder powerplant in the 1970s, and certain bastions of European motorcycling followed in the headlong pursuit of performance, Harley have persevered with their familiar form of propulsion. By slowly and quietly developing the large capacity, ohv V-twin, while everyone else was tinkering with three, four or even six pots, they displayed an unshakeable, some might say blinkered, confidence in their own beliefs.

The V-engine format has further advantages. Simplicity is one of them – naturally a twin has fewer moving parts than a complicated multi, so durability and reliability should be better, and routine maintenance can be tackled by riders themselves, if they prefer. No other engine layout gives such a short, stiff crankshaft, either. And when one cylinder is placed directly behind the other along the frame, the V-layout also gives maximum capacity for minimum engine width, so a greater angle of lean is theoretically possible. Having said that, few road-going Harleys tend to be scratched around in this fashion.

Harley-Davidson have also kept faith with their venerable V-twin because it can be slung low in the frame to give a lower centre of gravity. This gives better stability on the move, and a lower seat

At last the Sportster is catching up with bigger Harleys. Though the Evolution motor is torquey, the introduction of a five-speed gearbox on the 883 de-luxe and 1200 models is most welcome. Slicker shifting is now the norm, and revs are lower for any given road speed

height for comfort. Each motor employs just one carburettor to feed both cylinders, neatly sited in the 45° angle between the pots. It's much easier to keep in tune than a bank of four carbs, and uses less fuel.

Anyone who buys a Harley for its top-end performance then, or as a way of getting from A to B as fast as possible, is completely missing the point. The current 883cc, 1200cc aand 1340cc V-twins all deliver masses of torque low down in the rev range, to provide plenty of stomp away from the lights, or for overtaking manoeuvres. But the rev ceiling – 5200rpm for the bigger motors, and around 6000rpm for the smaller mills – is quite modest, due to the massive piston size. Typical acceleration, therefore, is only as fast as a good Jap 250cc, and their respective top speeds are also pretty close at around 100mph. But few Harley pilots ever find out, as braking is jokingly regarded as something of an optional extra.

No, riders choose a Harley-Davidson, and that characteristic V-twin feel and rumble, because they prefer riding their bikes at a steady pace. In other words, the V-twin performs optimally at moderate speeds – roughly in the 50–70mph bracket – and is therefore perfectly suited to American riding conditions. Over-enthusiastic revving of the engine and corner-to-corner holeshots are best left to the boy racers on their oriental projectiles. Life on a Harley is much more relaxed, thanks to the lazy beat of the big bore V-twin. So if a trip takes a little bit longer, that's fine – what's the rush? Sit back, enjoy the view, and listen to the music made by the best V-twin in the world.

Right
Harley-Davidson's most recent engine, introduced in 1984, is known as the V2 Evolution. That's because its bottom end is clearly descended from a V-twin design dating right back to 1936 – the 61E. The separate engine/gearbox design is still there but, unlike its predecessors, this one doesn't leak oil

Far right
Because the exhaust systems are both routed to the offside, the near side of the Evolution motor is relatively bare. However you can admire your reflection in the huge polished chaincase, here removed for servicing

Still surrounded by a conventional duplex tubular steel frame, the big V-twin of this Softail is a reminder of how many riders want their motorcycles to look elemental, with their insides on the outside. The motor is out there in the airstream to cool itself — and to show off its muscles, of course

Evolution engine has aluminium alloy heads and cylinders, the latter with iron liners, to permit greater and more even heat distribution. Harley have stuck with the 45 angle of the cylinders, even though this was a somewhat arbitrary choice

Shovelhead design of 74ci/1200cc capacity first appeared in 1966. From 1978 a larger 80ci/1340cc version, fitted with electronic ignition, became available and lasted until the engine was superseded in 1984

*Unlike Japanese bikes, no Harley
conceals its beautiful engine behind
sheets of fibreglass*

Sportsters

What was the best selling big bike in the USA at the start of the 1990s? The Ohio-built Honda Gold Wing perhaps, or one of the many across-the-frame Japanese multis? Nope – it was a genuine home-grown product and amazingly, one that had been around for well over thirty years!

Ever since 1957, Harley-Davidson enthusiasts have enjoyed the option of a budget-priced, entry-level model – the Sportster. In direct contrast to the mammoth full-dress tourers like the legendary Electra Glide, loaded up with every imaginable option and then some, the Sporster is motorcycling in its purest and simplest form.

In an age when two-wheelers have become unfathomably complex, particularly those from Japan, the Harley Sportster is like a throwback to an altogether more innocent era of motorcycles. The bike has been around for so long it's gone out of, and come back into, fashion. There are no frills or excess baggage on this lean machine – just a lightweight, powerful, and good handling package, designed to capture the very essence of riding pleasure.

Despite its marathon production run, the appearance of the Sportster has hardly changed. High handlebars loop over the classic peanut tank, perched as ever directly above the familiar V-shaped cylinders. Chrome abounds on the tiny headlamp, exhaust pipes, air cleaner and rear suspension units, complementing the polished alloy surfaces. A single seat is still fitted to the standard 883cc model, but a dual seat adorns the de-luxe and 1200cc versions.

The pared-down look might be constant, but the Sportster has been re-engineered of late to make it a viable modern motorcycle. Apart from the adoption of the Evolution motor back in 1986, the start of the '90s saw a fifth cog added to the gearbox, and a Kevlar belt drive system, similar to the big twins, for taking power to the rear wheel. Indeed, few parts from a mid-'80s Sportster would find their way onto the latest versions.

Though marginally quicker than the 'Glide – both in a straight line and through the twisty stuff – the sports emphasis of the Sportster is

What gives you the impression Harley-Davidson are proud of the five-speed transmission on their latest Sportster?

still something of a misnomer, in comparison with other makes of bike. Back in the '50s, however, things were far worse! For two decades after its introduction the Harley's agricultural mill, with an iron top-end, powered it somewhat slothfully about. All that changed with the fitting of the Evolution motor. With a return to the 883cc engine capacity in 1986, accompanied by an 1100cc variant, the Sportster has enjoyed a new lease of life.

Forget the Sportster if you wish to travel long distances in comfort. The tiny petrol tank, high bars, thinly padded seat and modest suspension all conspire against it. But for short blasts in the country or, better, cruising around the urban environment where people can admire your heroic profile, there's little to touch this bike. Because of its various limitations, the pose value of the Sportster has always been far more potent than the motorcycle itself. But the gap is narrowing, and for many this machine still represents the ideal economic entry point to the marque.

Above
I see no ships! 1970 version of XLH, residing in Harley museum at York, Pa, featured this unusual boattail seat/fender design. Otherwise it's pure Sportster. (Mac McDiarmid)

Right
A beach, a warm sunset and a 5-speed 1200 Sportster make a great photographic combination. Sport version with single seat – though there is nothing to stop the owner changing the look to a tourer with windshield, camel-back seat, saddlebags, etc – if the mood takes him. (David Goldman)

Screaming Eagle air cleaner is a common Sportster add-on. This owner has also fitted a steering damper, oil cooler and a sturdy linkage to switch the gear lever to the bike's offside

Even surrounded by acres of automotive sheetmetal, there's no mistaking the profile of the Sportster. The peanut tank, tiny headlamp, high bars and oval air cleaner mean just one thing

Left
Evo Sportster engines piled up to the factory ceiling make a mouthwatering sight for anybody who speaks Harley's language – that's torque with a capital T. There are four Sportster models, three with 883 engines, the same displacement as the first one in 1957, the fourth a serious 1200. (Mac McDiarmid)

Above
Latest Sportster engines have been criticised by some as having lost their grunt – mainly due to emasculation by emission regulations. As usual, there are ways and means round the problem . . .

Like the 1340cc bikes, top Sportsters
now enjoy the benefit of cleaner,
quieter belt drive to the rear wheel.
Meanwhile the cooking XLH and the
Hugger soldier on with dirty, power-
robbing chains

Pre-Evolution Sportster, known as the Ironhead, was made until 1985. Crankcases look similar but are not interchangeable. He's checking whether his candy paintwork is bluer than the ocean

British racer Nigel Gale campaigned his 883cc Sportster at Daytona, and won. The boots are nicely worn in. (David Goldman)

Road riders might treat their 883s with kid gloves, but there's no pussyfooting around when the production riders climb aboard their Sportsters to race. Knee pads are an essential item of kit. (David Goldman)

Customs & Cruisers

Pitched slap in-between the slimline Sportsters and the titanic tourers, Harley-Davidson continue to manufacture a series of big-bore motorcycles with a broad variety of sporting and cruising pretensions. Historically, the Milwaukee-based company have employed for some reason an often impenetrable system of multiple letters to designate different models, such as XLH for the Sportster, or the Electra Glide's FLHTC. In that context, the models here can be divided into the FXS/FLS variants, and the FXRs.

Thankfully the bikes are given a normal description beyond the mysterious letter configurations, so you'll find most aficionados refer to their Harleys as, say, a Low Rider or a Super Glide, rather than an FXRS or FXR. That's only right, because these things are much more than a cold piece of apparatus – Harleys have character by the ton.

Each and every Harley-Davidson is a somewhat elemental device, but broadly speaking the FXR bikes are contemporary-looking (for Harley, that is) designs with superb looks absolutely guaranteed to turn heads. First seen in 1977, the Low Rider wore rakish forks and, with its 27in seat height, a get-down riding position. Softails, on the other hand, exhibit a selection of traditional elements blended with up-to-date engineering – for many the best of both worlds of motorcycling.

Each range appeals to a cross-section of fundamentalist bikers – those who prefer a powerful engine they can see and feel at work, wrapped either in a set of components which make a statement about taste and style, or which make strong references to the company's unique heritage.

Take a look at the Softail's rear end, for instance. The back wheel appears rigidly mounted at a cursory glance, just like the famous Hardtail bikes of yesteryear. Actually there is a suspension system, placed horizontally under the gearbox. This ingenious solution imbues the Softail with a nostalgic appearance, yet features the comfort and wheel travel of a modern mount.

Lean back and enjoy the ride with highway footpegs. Lacking an open-face helmet and shades, the owner of this Softail Custom has that distinctly English weather look

Two bikes epitomise Harley-Davidson's philosophy in the 1990s – moving forward, certainly, but never forgetting where they've been. Like a two-wheeled time capsule, the spirit of the early dressers is captured in the FLSTC Heritage Softail Classic, which comes complete with clear screen plus a studded seat and saddlebags. Other makers build retro-bikes, too, but never like this. And only Harley could possibly make the FLSTF Fat Boy, which with its cast wheels makes a splendid virtue of its solidity.

The shape of things to come, again with strong links in the past, is also visible in the FXDB Sturgis – Harley-Davidson's latest metal masterpiece. It is quite fitting to name a bike after the world's greatest motorcycle gathering, now well past its 50th birthday. The new model, finished in all-black just like its 1980 namesake, boasts a newly introduced and virtually vibrationless Dyna Glide chassis – for the last decade other Harley models have sported a rubberised isolation system to reduce unwanted vibes. Though the Sturgis heralds a new era of smoothness for the marque, this machine, like its stablemates, still delivers the Harley goods.

This is Fat Boy country, so forget all that heroic scratching you've learned on other bikes. Shallow angles of lean are essential to avoid grounding the undercarriage. (David Goldman)

Right
Hustle the Fat Boy too hard and chances are you'll get squashed. Nice steady cruising is its forte, just fast enough for you to catch those admiring glances. (David Goldman)

Conventional rear suspension differentiates FXR-series bikes, like this Super Glide, from Softails

Looking the part on a Heritage Softail Classic, unencumbered with the distracting look of conventional rear shock absorbers. Smoking a cigarette while riding looks real cool, until you accidentally set the beard on fire . . .

98% of Harley riders are male, apparently, but this Heritage Softail Classic at speed has a female pilot. Classic model differs from regular Heritage by adding a screen, studded seat and saddlebags, a backrest for the passenger and a neat two-tone paint job. It's a combination that commands attention

Reintroduced for the '90s, the FXDB Sturgis looks similar to the ten-year-old model of the same name, but is radically different. Like the rest of the bike, the Evo engine is dressed in all-black, but the biggest news is the vibration-reducing Dyna Glide chassis.(David Goldman)

As Harley-Davidson moved into the 1990s, they decreed the new look was . . . fat! With solid wheels, deeply valanced mudguards and a ton of nostalgic styling elements, the FLSTF Fat Boy proved an instant hit. (David Goldman)

Evolution motor is a mass of evocative surfaces. In its first year of production, the Fat Boy's 1340cc engine wore these yellow highlights to lift the overall silver-grey paint scheme

FXRS Low Rider Convertible doubles up as a city or country mount. Quick-release couplings enable the windshield and saddlebags fitted as standard to be rapidly removed

Traditional-look chromed front dome on hub of Heritage Softail provides a panoramic view of your surroundings, but limits the braking department to a single disc

Look at all that chrome to polish, and that's before the nooks and crannies of the engine are contemplated. This Springer Softail is typically spotless, however. Many riders reckon on about four or five hours' riding to a solid hour of cleaning

Unmistakeable even from a block away. This Softail has been mildly customised with flyscreen, rev counter, medallion gas caps and fringed seat

Springer Softail, launched by Harley-Davidson in 1988, reintroduced a front suspension design absent from the motorcycle scene for decades

Outside the heavyweight tourers, the only Harley to wear a pukka fairing is the FXRT Sport Glide

Kings of the Highway

Solo or two-up, long distance trips demand a degree of protection from the elements, limousine-style comfort plus plenty of gear-toting capacity. In these regards, few bikes can match the FL Tourers. And one model in particular – the Electra Glide – is still America's symbolic King of the Highway.

The first FLH appeared in 1957, wearing a clear windshield to keep the worst of the breeze and bugs at bay, and leather saddlebags. 35 years on, the latest FLHTC Ultra boasts gadgets like a CB intercom integrated with a quality stereo system, digital clock, cigarette lighter and cruise control. Yet the bike's essential elements remain the same, with a big, lazy V-twin still providing tractor-like torque, and seating accommodation comfortable enough to come from Cadillac.

As with the company's lighter models, new technology has only been introduced to the FL range when Harley-Davidson engineers felt there was a definite advantage to be gained. For 1965, an electric starter was added to save perspiring owners kicking over the massive 1207cc motor, leading to the revered Electra Glide name. Where once there were very hot and hard-pressed drum brakes, triple discs now halt the third of a ton machine with reasonable efficiency, aided by a front suspension complete with anti-drive system.

The dawn of the 1980s saw a rubber-mounted engine to isolate vibrations from the rest of the bike, so that loose fillings and blurred vision need no longer be part of the Harley experience. Also at this time, a belt drive was introduced to transmit power to the rear wheel. This Kevlar-reinforced, toothed strip is, remarkably, cleaner than, and as durable as, a chain, yet lighter and slicker shifting than a shaft. Nor does it possess any of the unwanted torque characteristics associated with the latter system. In other words, a useful step forward.

Also launched at the turn of the '80s, to accompany the Electra Glide, came the Tour Glide model – the first ever Harley to sport a five-speed gearbox. Whereas the long-running FLHTC tourer enjoys

C'mon, gimme a real gradient! Torque of 1340cc V-twin will lug you up the mountainside with ease.
(Mac McDiarmid)

the benefit of a shapely fork-mounted fairing, that on the newer FLTC bike is larger, more angular, has twin headlights and is attached to the frame instead. Ultra variants of each model offer the highest specifications, but what all the Glides have in common is a saddle and passenger perch which are acclaimed as perhaps the most comfortable in the touring motorcycle industry.

It's always in Harley-Davidson's interests to keep links with the past, and the Glides manage that in many ways. Look, for example, at those full-coverage mudguards adorned with nostalgic trim. Even the familiar tank-top bump for the fuel cap and controls has been retained, though the main instrument cluster is fitted in the fairing. Now the radio and CB buttons occupy this traditional position.

Last but not least in the current FL line-up is the FLHS Sport model, which harks back to the first Harley tourers with its perspex screen and panniers. Shorn of many of the extras fitted to the full-dress brigade, the Sport is touring as originally intended. Whereas technologically sophisticated multi-cylinder bikes, spearheaded by the Honda Goldwing, have elevated travelling on two wheels to almost car-like efficiency and detachment – they'll be fitting an auto-pilot next – the timeless Harley Glides rumble on, never letting you forget you're travelling on a genuine motorcycle.

1340cc machine especially tailored for American police forces – the FXRP, here with the Houston PD. Note the large police speedometers giving a clear reading at speed without the need to look down too far for too long; a useful safety feature in that line of work

With a dry weight of around 750 lbs,
the Electra Glide has plenty of
directional stability in a straight line,
but is hardly in the Slingshot category
when bends are encountered.
Handling is predictable and steady on
faster, sweeping corners, providing
you don't press too hard. Low speed
manoeuvring through tight turns is
surprisingly good. (Mac McDiarmid)

Tour Glide Classic has a large frame-mounted fairing with dual headlights to distinguish it from the Electra Glide's fork-mounted number. (David Goldman)

Left
Seating accommodation on the FL tourers is probably the best in the entire motorcycle industry. Passengers enjoy a contoured backrest and a pair of personal speakers

Opposite
One look at those clouds and you might think it's Hog Heaven. Actually it's coastal fog creating atmosphere on Highway 1 in California.
(Mac McDiarmid)

Overleaf
Shovelhead-powered FLH Special Edition Electra Glide has panniers fitted, but omits full-dress fairing and luggage box. Note kickstart near rear cylinder exhaust pipe

Below
Tassles on this FLH steed reinforce the view of the biker as the modern American cowboy

Right
Three tourer pilots demonstrate you don't have to be a youthful desperado to ride a Harley

Right
You like creature comforts? Welcome aboard the cockpit of the Electra Glide. Cruise control is placed near the right-hand fork

Opposite
Additional weather protection for the legs is standard with the Ultra Classic versions of the Electra Glide and Tour Glide. Fibreglass panels are neatly integrated with the crash bars

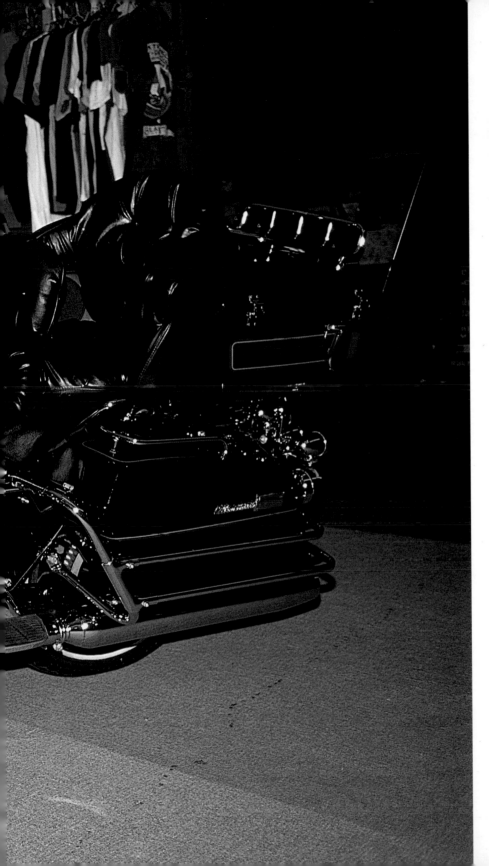

Above
Recent FL touring bikes feature all-round air damping with a simple but effective anti-dive system at the front. Suspension adjustment is simple – the handlebar acts as the air reservoir, with a valve by the left grip

Left
Full-dress, Harley style, encompasses bikes and riding gear. The Ultra Classic Electra Glide will pamper its rider with every cruising comfort including a CB intercom and cruise control. If there's any money left over, the range of clothing showing your allegiance to the marque is quite mind-blowing

Above
The Electra Glide in its element – no matter how long and straight the road, the Harley tourer eats it up with a lazy beat. (Mac McDiarmid)

Right
Dusk and another Electra Glide rolls into town to join the growing numbers of motorcycles lining the streets – welcome to Bike Week at Daytona Beach, Florida. (David Goldman)

People, Paint and Places

For 50 weeks in any year, Sturgis – a small, unassuming community by the Black Hills of South Dakota – is as subdued and sleepy as any other representative of small-town America. During the other fortnight, it shudders and throbs to the constant beat of thousands of lusty V-twin engines. Out on the streets, you can hardly move for Harley-Davidsons. This is the closest thing to Hog Heaven, for two weeks at least. Early August is when the largest motorcycle gathering on Earth takes place. Sturgis has been the host for the last 50 years.

From every corner of the States, and a string of countries too long to list, riders descend upon Sturgis for an orgy of revving, drinking, meeting, posing, ogling and just having a good time. Japanese machines aren't exactly run out of town, but it's better to park them round the back to avoid ridicule. Gathered here every year is the most colourful and dazzling array of Harleys you can imagine. Period. And it goes without saying that the folks who ride the machines into town make the eyes boggle just as much.

There's a certain irony in the well-worn, stereotyped image of the Harley rider as the wayward modern-day cowboy – someone out on the edge of society, an outlaw almost. Because those people charged with the task of catching the country's law infringers not only wear identical shades, they ride the same machines. Though oriental bikes have made inroads into many police fleets, Highway patrolmen still covet their Harley-Davidson mounts, and usually regard them as the most practical tool in a force's entire stable of vehicles.

Though infamous Harley-riding gangs still invade Sturgis, as they do other rallies, serious trouble seems to be a thing of the past. During the bike fortnight, there is plenty of partying, but only as many incidents as occur in other towns of similar size. The biggest danger to visitors and residents during the gathering is that of lack of sleep – the noise continues until around 4am or so, when even the most fanatical turn it in and get some shuteye.

Many bikers attend rallies just to eyeball the custom scene – to see who's done what to their bikes, as few examples remain as pure as

Life's a beach, at least at Daytona. Bikes, mainly Harleys, parade up and down the sandy strip all day, all week, with everybody checking out form

No place to hide, and almost no place to drink, because every watering hole for miles is packed with boisterous bikers

the factory intended for long. At Sturgis, Bike Week at Daytona Beach in March, or any of the numerous other H-D gatherings, you'll find every style, permutation, colour and hue of Harley under the sun. Harley riders treat their bikes as mobile canvases for their personal art, adding accessories or applying outrageous paint schemes to personalise their machines. Others adopt a more ambitious approach, radically altering the factory design both mechanically and aesthetically – if you'll pardon the pun, going the whole hog. The results are often sensational, sometimes hilarious, but invariably most professional. (The threat of EEC regulations on the other side of the Atlantic, designed to prevent just such customising, prompted a massive protest bike rally in London in July 1991).

Being a dedicated bunch, Harley owners think nothing of travelling a few hundred, or even a few thousand, miles to a meeting. Work is something done between rides, because quite simply, Harley-Davidson is more than a motorcycle – it's a way of life.

Come nightfall during Bike Week at Daytona Beach, the atmosphere is something else

Left
Daytona Beach welcomes bikers. For a whole week the place is transformed, reverberating to the rumble of countless V-twins. The machines and the people are both essential viewing

Right
Street art, Harley style. Good customising attracts a posse of appreciative onlookers every few seconds

Below right
Want to see some out-of-the-ordinary Harleys? Zoom along to Sturgis or Daytona and they'll be coming out of your ears. These two highly modified examples are typical of the extraordinary mechanical and cosmetic artistry on view every day of the week. (David Goldman)

Several outfits in the UK specialise in producing custom Harleys, including machines to individual customer specifications. Harley Street in deepest Suffolk claim the credit for this extraordinary Low Rider

This old Ironhead Sportster, though growing tatty in places, has been much loved. Look at the engraving on this rocker cover

Guns but no roses – that's the theme for this incredible Softail custom. The pistol in its holster is remarkable enough, but how about the shotgun silencer . . .

Above
Once the bike has been acquired, you'll need some gear. There's countless ways of displaying your allegiance to Harley, literally from tip to toe. Open face helmets look the part

Right
Apart from genuine Harley-Davidson accessories, a host of independent manufacturers produce custom items to hang on your bike. Chromed eagle-motif air cleaner covers are a popular choice

If this is the number of lights at the back, how many up front? Must be one powerful alternator. Nice plate

Mt Rushmore, which forms the basis for this high quality custom paint job is an appropriate subject, being close to Sturgis

Above
*Not all custom paint is done by the
specialists. Many owners dabble at
DIY, with varying degrees of success*

Right
*Guaranteed on a Harley Springer
Softail; double eagle on the caps*

Above

Eagle iron. This beautifully customised Springer Softail makes its neighbouring Goldwing look drab in the extreme. Even the engines' pushrod tubes have received exquisitely detailed attention

Left

Lovely detail customising on this petrol tank includes zany stripey paint, HOG medallion gas caps and a couple of wild faces peering eerily from the speedo

Left
A few prefer their Harleys just as the factory made them, but most seek a more personal identity for their bikes. This Shovelhead sports extra lights, fishtail silencers and an unusual but striking brown paintwork

Above
Screens are for looking through, sure, but they're another potential area for customising, so why not add another eagle? Not surprisingly, H-D prefer you to buy aftermarket trimmings from H-D dealers

HD EVO – a neat plate but not one to impress the British copper

Hollywood Harleys congregate by Carneys – an old Union Pacific railroad car converted into a trendy hamburger joint. (Mac McDiarmid)

Left
Membership of the Harley Owners Group tends to last for years, if not a lifetime

Overleaf
HOG membership is all about riding and socialising. Most chapters are pretty active, with events occurring every month if not every week. These riders are members of the Hou-Tex (Houston, Texas) chapter out on a gentle 150-mile Saturday run

Some female Harley riders like to
dress conservatively, but this isn't one
of them. A sparkling black Springer
Softail with gold detailing makes a
perfect travelling picture frame for
this Florida golden girl

It's regarded as ungentlemanly to talk about a lady's age, but Dot won't mind me giving some indication. She's not a million miles off the 80 mark, and a founding member of the women's motorcycle group in Florida, soon to celebrate its 50th anniversary. Here she pulls her Heritage Softail off the highway to park at Daytona – a regular haunt. Why the pink bike? Dot was fed up with her husband borrowing the Harley, so she hit upon the idea of painting it a feminine colour. Hubby hasn't touched it since!

Right
Hog dog. This hairy pilot tries hard to look cool in an all-yellow outfit to match the bike

Left

What do these two machines have in common? That's right, the decrepit MkI Ford Escort in the background and the gleaming 1989 Heritage Softail have (more or less) the same size engine; and they're the only machines in this book residing in Medina, Western Australia. Formerly a diehard Norton and Triumph man, owner Chico Holmes traded in the best of British for his first Harley a few years back when he decided he was getting too old for kick-starts! (Chico is the uncle of an Osprey editor – and the picture was taken by the editor's Dad, so we didn't have much choice but to put it in)

Above

Cruising on the beach – a great way to top up the tan, but mind the bare flesh doesn't touch those exhaust pipes

Left
As you might expect, Hollywood has its fair share of Harley riders. Here the boys adopt suitable poses outside Johnny Rockets' eatery. Disappointingly, the tyres aren't chromed. (Mac McDiarmid)

Above
Daytona was great. Loads of Harleys. And I met this really nice guy, Mom

Above
*All smiles from this tattoed lady
Harley rider. With infamous gangs in
close proximity, you might think
rallies are dangerous places, but
trouble rarely occurs and the
atmosphere is like one big party*

Right
*Two gentlemen exchange ideas on the
propagation of houseplants. The
machines (FLSTC Heritage Softail
Classic left, FLST Heritage Softail
right both minus screens) are
relatively accessory-free, with
'standard' paint finishes; but if their
owners wanted a change, they could
browse through the H-D dealer's stock
and come up with anything from a
custom handlebar clamp in solid brass
to a chrome perforated shield for the
muffler*

Left
*This bright yellow Springer shows
exactly why riders like Harley-
Davidsons – the fusion between older
and modern technologies, and the
bikes' earthy quality. The big V-twin is
basically a 50-year-old design, as is
the front suspension. But a belt drive
transmits power to the rear wheel*

Above
*Harleys from America, Canada and all
over Europe assemble at a UK rally in
Cheltenham*

Let the Fat Boy roll. The bike, I mean –
not the rider. The FLSTF glories in its
own solidity like a Sumo wrestler

Highway pegs provide a more relaxed method of travelling, and enhance the Easy Rider image

Shades, a red headband, stubble, ripped denim and a tattoo – this Harley rider must be an accountant. (Mac McDiarmid)

Eagles dominate these small but significant ways to express your feelings in little lumps of moulded metal

Pre-1985 Ironhead Sportster hits town.
If you consider the fact that this is an
'old' machine – on a Japanese design
timescale, a dinosaur – you can
quickly see that the Harley identity is
always preserved

Don't search for this one in the manufacturers' catalogue! For the rider who builds up a powerful thirst on a ride, taking a personal supply looks like a good idea

Left

Belt drive to transmit power to the rear wheel was introduced to the Harley range in 1981. The toothed Kevlar-reinforced belt is a clever piece of engineering, as it is lighter, simpler and absorbs less power than shaft drive. Yet compared to a chain, it is quieter, gives smoother gear shifts and requires fewer adjustments. Its strength is also sufficient to stand the huge torque of the 1340cc motor, so no more cracks about rubber bands, please

Right

The novel front suspension of the FXSTS Springer usually demands attention, but with this dramatic red and yellow special paintwork the bike becomes a real headturner

The Harley Owners Group, usually abbreviated to HOG, is big-time in America and has spread to Europe. The growing membership now exceeds 130,000. Social gatherings and discounts off accessories are just two of the reasons to join up

Electra Glide by Harley-Davidson,
headwear by Calvin Klein

HOG member. Actually, aftermarket accessory ref. 99418-88V: 'all four feet drilled and tapped. Hardware included.'

A welcome sight if you've ridden from New York on a coast-to-coast trip. A Harley sweeps round a bend on Twin Peaks, Market Street, with the city of San Francisco sprawling ahead. (Mac McDiarmid)

The scale of Yosemite's landscape is sometimes hard to appreciate. To gauge the size of the lump of granite this Harley is swooping past, look at the size of the trees on top of it!
(Mac McDiarmid)

They say smoking is bad for you, but who cares when you've just ridden a couple of hundred miles. The Low Rider Convertible and Electra Glide Classic take a breather in Missouri. (Mac McDiarmid)

Above
Fat Boy, with relatives, Disney's Epcot Center

Right
Highway patrolman Tom Barnes radios in to Houston police HQ.